This book is dedicated to the memory of LoDema and DeWitt Daniel, about whom these family stories are told. Many of the stories may have been magnified or altered by the passing years, but one thing remains constant: The lives of LoDema and Dewitt Daniel glorified God.

A TELL-WELL BOOK

Teach me to Pray

By Bill and Bernard Martin

The John C. Winston Company

PHILADELPHIA · TORONTO

CONTENTS

FOREWORD

ONE of the great privileges of man is the enjoyment of his children. One of the great tragedies of man is that he discovers this fact too late and takes advantage of it too little.

In this mad world of ours where wars bloody the earth and misunderstandings make havoc of homes, we parents are summoned to preserve the beautiful things of life and are challenged to make this a better world tomorrow by training our children today.

For it is not by accident that children become good men and women. Long, patient, careful training in the ways of life, instilling gentleness and kindness, is necessary to make our little ones into the kind of people who can insure a decent world tomorrow and the day after.

Blessed is the home where both mother and father are close enough to their children to guide them naturally into "the life that is life indeed." To be a "Dad" whose homecoming is eagerly awaited at the end of the day; to be a "Mother" who has learned to live and love and laugh and work and play with her boys and girls—these are the immeasurable joys for parents that help build faith and confidence and security in children's lives. There would be little juvenile delinquency if all parents were thus child-minded.

One of the refreshing signs in the field of juvenile education today is the work of Bill and Bernard Martin, two fine young men of Kansas City. In all of their books they tend to bring children and parents together into family storytelling and family reading, age-old pleasures out of which come a joy of reading and a love for good stories from life, adventure, and the Bible. "Teach Me To Pray" is both a winning story and a great teaching on prayer. Wise parents will use it as a stimulus for serving the individual spiritual needs of their children.

DR. RALPH W. SOCKMAN
Minister, Christ Church, Methodist
New York

Our Family
PRAYS

Lord, teach us to pray.—LUKE 11:1.

MANY years ago I lived with my father and mother and brothers and sisters on a pretty Kansas farm. Each of us had his chores to do, for there were cows to milk, chickens and pigs to feed, fields to plow and plant and harvest, and a big house and family to care for. We worked from sunrise until dark, but no matter how busy we were, Father took time after breakfast each morning for family worship.

Sometimes Father read from the Bible and offered the family prayer; sometimes, Mother. Sometimes we children prayed, each taking his turn to thank God for the good gifts He had given us.

The prayers we children offered were short and simple, but sincere. Like all growing children who always are hungry, we enjoyed telling God daily: "We are glad for the good food we have, God. Thank you. Amen." In spring when the fields were white with flowers, we liked to pray: "We are glad for the daisies that grow in the meadow, God. Tomorrow we shall pick some for Grandmother. Amen." And a favorite prayer of ours was: "God, we are glad for our mother and father. Help us love them more today than we did yesterday. Amen."

God has given you many wonderful gifts: your home, your mother and daddy, and a big, beautiful world to enjoy. What other gifts has God given you? Would you like to tell God how glad you are for your mother and father?

FAMILY PRAYER: *O God, we are glad that You are in our home today to bind us together into one joyful family. Amen.*

FIRST DAY OF THE MONTH

Why Do We
PRAY

And the glory of the Lord came into the house.—EZEKIEL 43:4.

ONE morning at breakfast we were surprised to see that Mother had placed a lovely, pink rose beside each plate. Her eyes twinkled as she greeted us with a round of "good morning" kisses.

"What is this, Deemie?" Father asked suspiciously. "Is this someone's birthday?"

Mother laughed gaily. "This isn't a birthday, but it is a special occasion. As I cooked breakfast this morning, I thought what a great privilege it is to have a fine, wonderful family to love and care for. Often I forget to say it; but from now on, I'm going to take time each day to tell you how much I love you. Today I put the roses by the plates to remind you of my love."

Often we fail to tell each other of our love. Don't you think it would be fun to tell each other every morning that we are glad for our family and for our home? God, too, is a member of our family, so we should remember to include Him.

Whenever we tell God how much we love Him and how much we enjoy the good gifts He has given us, it makes us feel warm and happy inside, and it makes God happy, too. Prayer is talking to God. Prayer is also listening to God. We do not listen to God with our ears for God does not talk to us with words that we can hear. We listen to God with our mind because He sends thoughts into our mind to help us in every need. Would you like to tell God how much you love Him and how glad you are that He is a member of our family?

FAMILY PRAYER: *O God, who made heaven and earth and all that is good and lovely, help us to delight in each other and in Your abiding love. Amen.*

SECOND DAY OF THE MONTH

When Do We
PRAY

Evening, and morning, and at noon, will I pray
. . . and He shall hear my voice.—Psalms 55:17.

WE SELDOM missed a service at our little, white frame church, although it was four miles from home. In fair weather, Father hitched our mules, Sugar and Coffee, to the buggy and we bumped along the rough roads to church. In winter, when ice and snow blocked the roads, we took a short cut across the fields, riding in an old spring wagon that Father converted into a sled.

One of the few times that we missed going to church was a day of a heavy rain. The roads were impassable. I was very unhappy because I would not be in church to offer a prayer that I had learned for the occasion.

"Would you like to say your prayer now?" asked Mother.

"God probably wouldn't hear it," I fretted. "It isn't church time yet."

"Any time is a time for prayer. God is always listening."

While Mother and Father stood at my side on that early Sunday morning, I offered my prayer; and from the happy feeling I had inside me, I know that God heard it.

How many times a day should we pray? We should pray as often as we feel the need to pray. It does not greatly matter whether we pray silently or aloud. It does not matter whether we pray memorized prayers or make them up ourselves. What does matter is that we mean what we say to God with all our heart; that we feel His presence within us and let His thoughts fill our mind. Would you like to pray now, and thank God for our church and for our home?

FAMILY PRAYER: *We praise You, O God. We acknowledge You in all that we say and do. Amen.*

THIRD DAY OF THE MONTH

We Pray For
ONE ANOTHER

Thou shalt love thy neighbour as thyself.—LEVITICUS 19:18.

"HERE comes company! Here comes company!" were shouts of joy at our house.

Perhaps it was a schoolmate coming for a game of ball or for a jaunt to the creek. Perhaps it was our cousins, who had come from a distant town to spend the week with us. But no matter who came, we gave our visitors an enthusiastic welcome.

What good times we had with our guests, riding our ponies to the field, sliding down the half-built haystacks, and playing in the big barn. Sometimes we sat in the shade listening to Mother tell about the kind farmers who had given her fresh water, milk, eggs, and butter, when she was a little girl traveling across the plains in a moving wagon.

"The farmers welcomed everyone who passed," Mother commented.

"I wish some traveler would come here so we could help him," my brother said.

"You don't have to wait for a traveler," Mother explained. "You can start now by finding ways of caring for the needs of others. That is the secret of being a good neighbor."

Who are your "neighbors"? In what ways can you help them? Would you like to ask God to help you find some new ways of making your neighbors happy?

FAMILY PRAYER: *We are glad, dear God, for our friends and neighbors, and we are happy that we can serve them. Amen.*

FOURTH DAY OF THE MONTH

We Pray For
GOD'S LOVE

He shall feed his flock like a shepherd,
He shall gather the lambs in his arm, and
carry them in his bosom.—ISAIAH 40:11

FATHER called early one morning: "Children, come quickly. I need your help. The cattle are out."

We worked for several hours herding the cows and calves back into the pasture. Then Father mended the break in the fence, and we hurried to the house where Mother had breakfast waiting.

For our family worship that morning, Father read from the Bible a story that always has been my favorite. It told of a good shepherd who cared tenderly for his sheep; but one night, on returning home, he counted one sheep missing.

Without waiting for help or food, the brave shepherd went back alone into the dark, dangerous mountains where wild animals roamed. After a long search, the shepherd found his lamb caught in a bramble. Lifting the lamb gently, he laid it on his shoulders and carried it home. And great was the rejoicing when the shepherd returned with the lost lamb.

God is our shepherd. Night and day He watches over us and cares for us. Would you like to thank God for His love for us? (Read the 23rd Psalm.)

FAMILY PRAYER: *Every day will we bless You, O God. We will praise Your name forever and ever. Amen.*

FIFTH DAY OF THE MONTH

We Pray For
OUR DAILY NEEDS

My God shall supply all your need.—PHILIPPIANS 4:19.

MY SISTER Jane came home from school one day asking for a new pair of shoes. "I need them, Father," she insisted.

Father examined Jane's shoes and said, "Your shoes are not worn. They will last for some time."

"But I want some new brown shoes, just like the kind that Dorothy wears," pleaded Jane.

"Well, we can't get you brown shoes tonight," Father explained. "You won't mind wearing these old shoes tomorrow, will you?"

"I suppose not," Jane answered weakly.

"And if we can't go to the store tomorrow, I imagine that you could wear these old shoes until day after tomorrow, don't you?"

"I suppose so," agreed my sister.

"You see, Jane," Father chuckled, "you want some new shoes, but you don't necessarily need them. 'Wanting' and 'needing' are two different things."

What are our daily needs? (Home or shelter, food, clothing, and God's love.) God knows what we need even before we ask Him, but often we are selfish in wanting more than we really need. Can you make up a prayer asking God to help you not to want more than your share?

FAMILY PRAYER: *Dear God, help us to know what we should pray for, and to ask only for what is good for us. Amen.*

SIXTH DAY OF THE MONTH

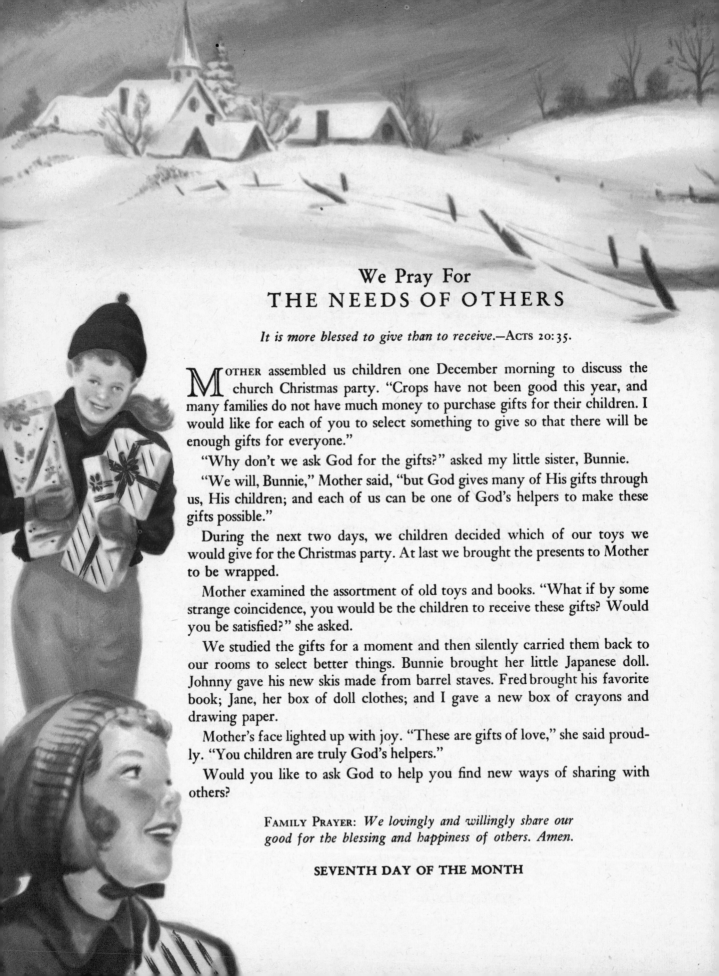

We Pray For
THE NEEDS OF OTHERS

It is more blessed to give than to receive.—ACTS 20:35.

MOTHER assembled us children one December morning to discuss the church Christmas party. "Crops have not been good this year, and many families do not have much money to purchase gifts for their children. I would like for each of you to select something to give so that there will be enough gifts for everyone."

"Why don't we ask God for the gifts?" asked my little sister, Bunnie.

"We will, Bunnie," Mother said, "but God gives many of His gifts through us, His children; and each of us can be one of God's helpers to make these gifts possible."

During the next two days, we children decided which of our toys we would give for the Christmas party. At last we brought the presents to Mother to be wrapped.

Mother examined the assortment of old toys and books. "What if by some strange coincidence, you would be the children to receive these gifts? Would you be satisfied?" she asked.

We studied the gifts for a moment and then silently carried them back to our rooms to select better things. Bunnie brought her little Japanese doll. Johnny gave his new skis made from barrel staves. Fred brought his favorite book; Jane, her box of doll clothes; and I gave a new box of crayons and drawing paper.

Mother's face lighted up with joy. "These are gifts of love," she said proudly. "You children are truly God's helpers."

Would you like to ask God to help you find new ways of sharing with others?

FAMILY PRAYER: *We lovingly and willingly share our good for the blessing and happiness of others. Amen.*

SEVENTH DAY OF THE MONTH

We Pray For
GUIDANCE

*Trust in the Lord with all thy heart, and lean not upon
thine own understanding. In all thy ways acknowledge
Him, and He will direct thy path.*—PROVERBS 3:5-6.

Two roads led from our home to the little village where we did our week-
ly trading. The road that led up a hill along higher ground was shorter
than the other; but it was not so pretty as the lower road which wound leis-
urely through a wooded valley.

As we neared the fork in the road, Father would ask, "Which way shall
we take today?" He permitted us children to choose. Sometimes the road we
selected was rough or muddy or windy or hot, and we children wished that
we had chosen the other way.

"You never know what you might have found on the other road," Father
replied. "Perhaps a bridge is out or the way is rough with rocks. You have
made your choice. Now let us enjoy it to the fullest."

Every day we make many choices: the friends we play with, the books
we read, the words we speak, the use of our play time. We cannot expect
to make wise choices unless we trust in God and ask His help. Would you
like to ask God to guide you in all the things you do today?

FAMILY PRAYER: *Guide us, O God, that we may enjoy
each day and its blessings. Amen.*

EIGHTH DAY OF THE MONTH

We Pray For
LOVE

Love is patient and kind; love is not jealous or boastful; it is not arrogant or rude. Love does not insist on its own way; it is not irritable or resentful; it does not rejoice at wrong, but rejoices in the right. Love bears all things, endures all things. Love never ends.—I CORINTHIANS 13:4-8.

FATHER never had much "ready cash" when we were young except from the sale of wheat and corn. We knew that whenever Father took a load of grain to market in Kansas City, he would return with a sizable amount of money. We also knew that he would return with a gift for each one of us.

After one of Father's trips to Kansas City, we children awakened to find gifts at the foot of our beds one morning. Father had brought Johnny a bicycle. He had brought the rest of us sacks of oranges and bananas and grapes—delicacies that we could not find in our village store.

All of us rejoiced that Johnny had received a bicycle. He had wanted it for a long, long time, and he needed it to run errands to the village and to the neighbors.

We children knew that regardless of the size or value of the gifts, Father loved each of us the same. We also knew that as Father could afford it, he would get for each of us in turn the things we especially longed for and needed.

All people do not have or need the same things, because God has made each of us different with different needs and desires. Some of our friends have more and will continue to have more than we do; but in our love for our friends, we rejoice in their gifts, whether we receive anything or not. Can you make up a prayer asking God to help you love your friends, even when they receive more than you do?

FAMILY PRAYER: *We thank You, dear God, for all of our friends and neighbors, and we rejoice in the good that comes to them. Amen.*

NINTH DAY OF THE MONTH

We Pray To Be
HELPFUL

They helped everyone his neighbour.—ISAIAH 41:6.

ABRAHAM LINCOLN was my great Grandfather's friend. When the young Mr. Lincoln was on a surveying trip through Illinois, he stayed at Grandfather's house. Therefore, Grandfather followed with keen interest the man who later became one of the great presidents of our country.

Grandfather knew many stories about Mr. Lincoln. One concerned a little bird.

While riding horseback along a country lane with some friends, Abraham Lincoln saw a little bird that had fallen from its nest. Dismounting from his horse, Mr. Lincoln put the tiny bird back into the tree where it would be safe.

"Why do you waste time doing this?" laughed his friends.

"I would not have felt right if I had passed without helping the little bird," Mr. Lincoln answered. "I feel much better for having done it."

How can you help: a boy who is lost, a lonely person, your mother, your church, a stray kitten? Would you like to tell God that you are glad when you can be helpful to your friends and neighbors?

FAMILY PRAYER: *We thank You, dear God, for making our lives bright and happy by showing us ways to be kind and helpful to others. Amen.*

TENTH DAY OF THE MONTH

5040

We Pray For
COURAGE

Be strong and of a good courage; fear not nor be afraid . . .
for the Lord thy God, He it is that doth go with thee;
He will not fail thee, nor forsake thee.—DEUT. 31:6.

A HEAVY spring rain washed a deep gully across our country road, and the men of the community built a wooden bridge over it. Being made of wide planks, the new bridge had a hollow sound; and our team of mules, Sugar and Coffee, refused to cross it.

"This is just a foolish fear," Father insisted. "Sugar and Coffee must learn that nothing about this bridge will harm them."

Soon, Father found a way to teach the mules to cross the span. When a neighbor came down the road in his spring wagon, Father followed him, driving our team of mules so close behind that the mules' heads extended over the bed of the wagon ahead of them and they could not see the ground. Before they realized it, Sugar and Coffee had followed the wagon over the bridge. From that time forward, they were not afraid to cross it.

All of us have "foolish fears" that prove to be nothing when we face them. There is nothing to fear in darkness; God planned the night so that we can rest. We should not be afraid to meet a new child in the neighborhood; he may become our best friend. We should not be afraid to be alone; it is an opportunity to talk with God and to explore His wonderful world. Would you like to ask God to help you have courage at times when you are afraid?

FAMILY PRAYER: *You are our strength and our courage,*
dear God. There is nothing for us to fear. Amen.

ELEVENTH DAY OF THE MONTH

We Pray For
SERVICE

By love serve one another.—GALATIANS 5:13.

WE LIGHTED our farm home with oil lamps because we didn't have electricity in those days. Each morning Mother took a great pride in cleaning the lamp chimneys until they were bright and shiny, but that was one task that I disliked totally.

"You should be glad we have lamps to clean," Mother tried to explain. "How much worse it was when Grandfather was a boy. His home was lighted with candles because there were no lamps in those days, and it was Grandfather's job to make the candles. What a long, tedious job it was!

"First, he inserted a string into each candle mold to make the wick. Then he melted the tallow to pour into the molds. When the tallow hardened, he removed the candles from the molds without breaking them. Making candles for the entire household took hours of Grandfather's time. Yet I heard him say many times that he was happy that he could serve his family in this manner."

After Mother's talk, I tried to be more cheerful when I had to clean the lamps; but I thought it would be more fun to watch Grandfather make the candles.

God wants each of us to be helpful. What can you do to serve (1) your family, (2) your friends, (3) your teachers, and (4) your church? Would you like to ask God to help you find new ways of helping others?

FAMILY PRAYER: *Dear God, help us find new joy in all the work we do today. Amen.*

TWELFTH DAY OF THE MONTH

We Pray For

OBEDIENCE

*Children, obey your parents in everything, for this
pleases the Lord.*—COLOSSIANS 4:20.

HELPING Mother wash the dishes was one of Jane's daily chores, but on
one hot July noon Jane slipped away and hid under the grapevines
that grew in our back yard. There, in the dark, cool shade, Jane stretched
out to watch a dragonfly darting in and out of "her castle." Mother called,
but her voice seemed so far away that my sister didn't bother to answer.

When Jane eased back into the kitchen an hour later, you can imagine her
surprise at finding the table still laden with dirty dishes.

"I'm glad you're back, Jane," Mother called pleasantly from the living
room. "I have other things to do today, so I had to leave the dishes for you."

Because the food on the dishes had dried and because the dishwater had
cooled, Jane spent all afternoon finishing her job. But no one scolded her.
There was no need. She had learned her lesson.

Every day you are asked to help others. What tasks do your parents assign
to you? Do you always obey? Do you feel happy when you fail to do what
your parents and teachers ask you to do? Would you like to ask God to help
you obey when your help is needed?

FAMILY PRAYER: *O God, fill our hearts with love and
understanding that we may cheerfully do whatever we
are called upon to do. Amen.*

THIRTEENTH DAY OF THE MONTH

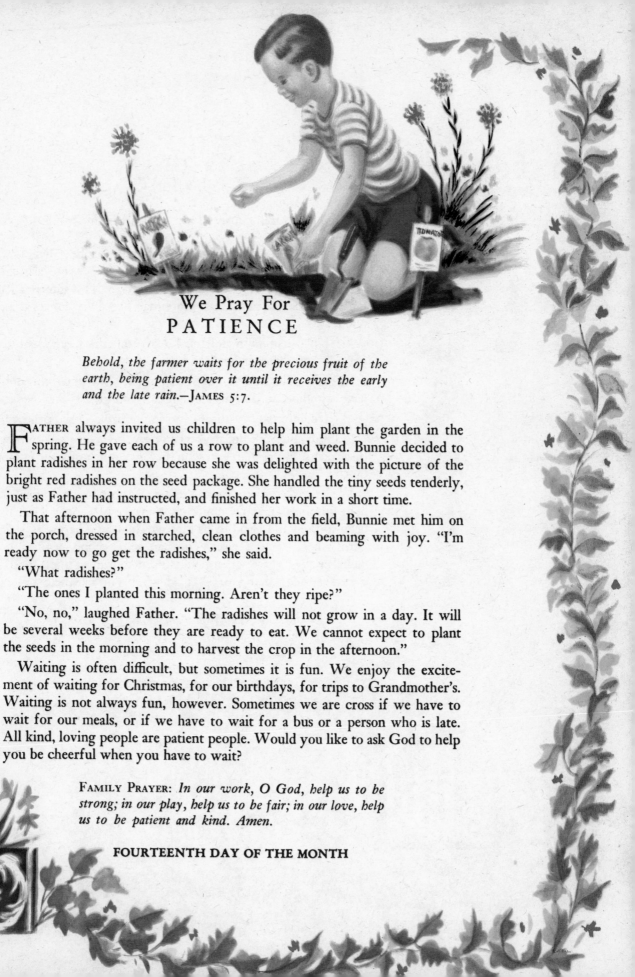

We Pray For
PATIENCE

Behold, the farmer waits for the precious fruit of the earth, being patient over it until it receives the early and the late rain.—JAMES 5:7.

FATHER always invited us children to help him plant the garden in the spring. He gave each of us a row to plant and weed. Bunnie decided to plant radishes in her row because she was delighted with the picture of the bright red radishes on the seed package. She handled the tiny seeds tenderly, just as Father had instructed, and finished her work in a short time.

That afternoon when Father came in from the field, Bunnie met him on the porch, dressed in starched, clean clothes and beaming with joy. "I'm ready now to go get the radishes," she said.

"What radishes?"

"The ones I planted this morning. Aren't they ripe?"

"No, no," laughed Father. "The radishes will not grow in a day. It will be several weeks before they are ready to eat. We cannot expect to plant the seeds in the morning and to harvest the crop in the afternoon."

Waiting is often difficult, but sometimes it is fun. We enjoy the excitement of waiting for Christmas, for our birthdays, for trips to Grandmother's. Waiting is not always fun, however. Sometimes we are cross if we have to wait for our meals, or if we have to wait for a bus or a person who is late. All kind, loving people are patient people. Would you like to ask God to help you be cheerful when you have to wait?

FAMILY PRAYER: *In our work, O God, help us to be strong; in our play, help us to be fair; in our love, help us to be patient and kind. Amen.*

FOURTEENTH DAY OF THE MONTH

We Pray For
GIVING

God loves a cheerful giver.—II CORINTHIANS 9:7.

WHEN the people of our community decided that a new church was needed, Father and others were asked to help raise money for the building program. This interested us children who had never seen more than five silver dollars at any one time.

"If I had a million dollars, I'd give all the money for the church," my brother Fred said.

"That would be fine," replied Father, "but since you don't have a million dollars, how much can you give?"

"I have only twenty-three cents in my bank," Fred protested.

"I know, my son. But if you can't give some of your twenty-three cents, I'm certain you wouldn't give much of your million dollars."

We are asked many times during the year to give money to help hospitals, schools, churches, and needy people. God has been so kind and good to us that we should be happy to share with others. If you wish, you can start saving pennies and nickels now to give when help is needed. Can you tell God in a prayer today that you are glad when you can help others?

FAMILY PRAYER: *We thank You, dear God, for Your bountiful gifts, and we give to others generously as we have received. Amen.*

FIFTEENTH DAY OF THE MONTH

We Pray For
CHILDREN

*Then He folded the children in His arms, and
placing His hands on them, gave them His blessing.*
—MARK 10:16.

MOTHER'S cousin, Olive, who was a missionary to Japan,
came to stay with us a few days when she returned to
America on a visit. We children surrounded her to hear the
stories of the Japanese and the Japanese children. Cousin Olive
also told us many things about the work of missionaries, but the
story we remember best concerned a missionary doctor.

The doctor had been working without sleep for many days in
a small Japanese village that was stricken with a plague of illness.
The doctor cared for the sick until he was so tired that he knew
he could not continue longer without rest.

"I am going to my room to sleep," the doctor told his helpers.
"Do not awaken me until morning."

The doctor then retired to his room, but in a moment he returned to add: "Do not awaken me—unless a little child should
need me."

God loves all people, especially little children, and He has
given them wonderful gifts, regardless of their race or color.
Would you like to ask God to help you love *all* children everywhere, just as He does?

FAMILY PRAYER: *Father, we thank You that Your
love includes all Your children everywhere. Amen.*

SIXTEENTH DAY OF THE MONTH

We Pray For
GOOD DEEDS

*Goodness and mercy shall follow me all the days
of my life.*—PSALMS 23:6.

BETWEEN the apple trees in the orchard, Father planted rows of wheat and rye, making a favorite place for the chickens to feed and the pigs to pasture. The long rows of dark green plants also made a favorite place for us children to play hide-and-go-seek.

We younger children ran far out into the rye, where the plants were taller than our heads. We thought we were so well hidden that Fred would never find us. But in less time than it had taken us to hide, Fred would catch us.

What we didn't realize was that Fred never had any difficulty in seeing exactly where we had gone. As we passed through the rye, we brushed aside the tender stalks, leaving a well-marked path for him to follow.

Often a stranger will say, "Oh, yes. I know you. You are the kind friend who came to visit Lynn when she was sick." Or perhaps your new teacher will say, "I've heard of you. You are the student who reads so well." No matter where you go, you leave marks along your path that show the kind of boy or girl you are. Would you like to ask God to help you remember to do at least one good deed every day?

FAMILY PRAYER: *We try, dear God, to do our
share of good and kindness everywhere. Amen.*

SEVENTEENTH DAY OF THE MONTH

We Pray For
CONTENTMENT

Be content with what you have.—HEBREWS 13:5.

DURING our childhood days farmers had plenty of food but little money. Therefore, Mother always taught us children to be content with what we had; and, for the most part, I cannot remember wanting for anything, except a carriage.

Our neighbors had just purchased a grand, new buggy with yellow wheels, red shafts, black leather seats, and yellow fringe on top. To me, life would never be complete unless we had a carriage just like it.

"But we don't need a new buggy," Mother explained.

"Our carriage isn't so pretty as theirs," I insisted.

"You will always be associated with people who have more than you have, who know more than you know, whose clothes are finer than yours. But you also will be associated with people who have less than you have, who know less than you know, whose clothes are not so fine as yours. It is not the people who *have* the best of things, but the people who *make* the best of things that get the most out of life. We must learn to be content with what we have," Mother explained.

If God had planned for all of us to be the same, He would have started by making us all alike. It would be a dull world if everyone looked and acted and thought alike, don't you agree? Would you like to tell God that we are grateful for the gifts He has given us?

FAMILY PRAYER: *O God, help us to delight in simple things and to rejoice in the richness of Your blessings. Amen.*

EIGHTEENTH DAY OF THE MONTH

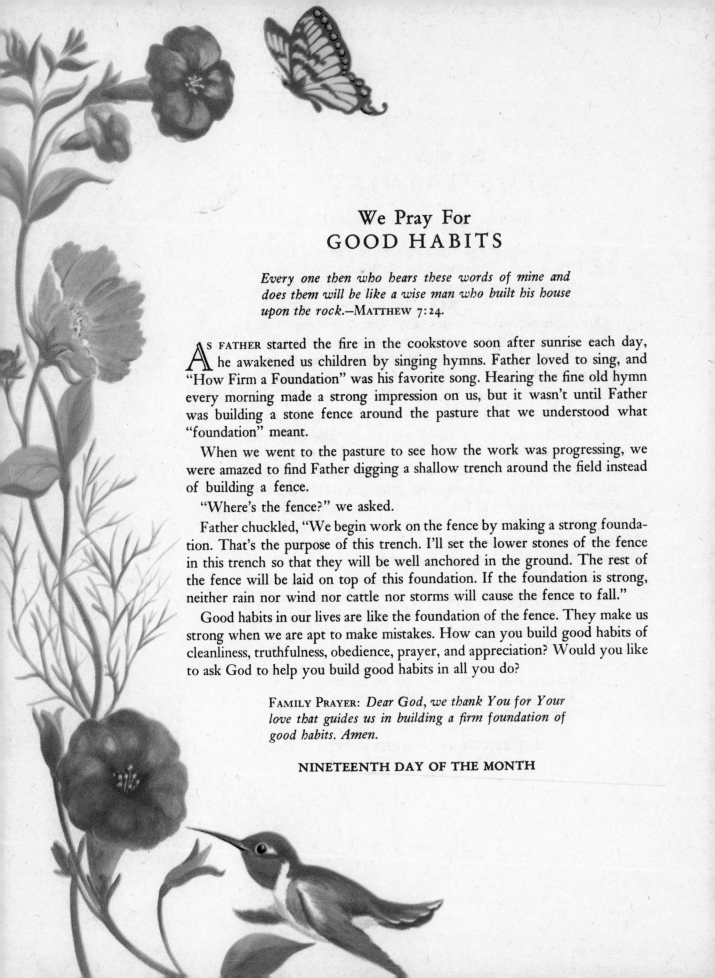

We Pray For
GOOD HABITS

*Every one then who hears these words of mine and
does them will be like a wise man who built his house
upon the rock.*—MATTHEW 7:24.

As FATHER started the fire in the cookstove soon after sunrise each day,
he awakened us children by singing hymns. Father loved to sing, and
"How Firm a Foundation" was his favorite song. Hearing the fine old hymn
every morning made a strong impression on us, but it wasn't until Father
was building a stone fence around the pasture that we understood what
"foundation" meant.

When we went to the pasture to see how the work was progressing, we
were amazed to find Father digging a shallow trench around the field instead
of building a fence.

"Where's the fence?" we asked.

Father chuckled, "We begin work on the fence by making a strong foundation. That's the purpose of this trench. I'll set the lower stones of the fence
in this trench so that they will be well anchored in the ground. The rest of
the fence will be laid on top of this foundation. If the foundation is strong,
neither rain nor wind nor cattle nor storms will cause the fence to fall."

Good habits in our lives are like the foundation of the fence. They make us
strong when we are apt to make mistakes. How can you build good habits of
cleanliness, truthfulness, obedience, prayer, and appreciation? Would you like
to ask God to help you build good habits in all you do?

FAMILY PRAYER: *Dear God, we thank You for Your
love that guides us in building a firm foundation of
good habits. Amen.*

NINETEENTH DAY OF THE MONTH

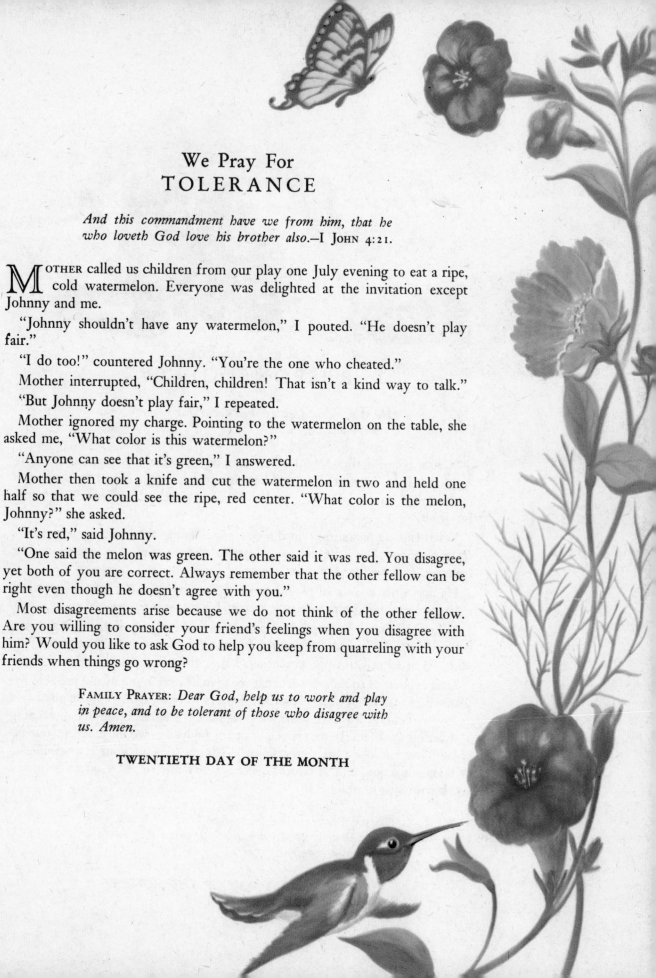

We Pray For
TOLERANCE

And this commandment have we from him, that he who loveth God love his brother also.—I JOHN 4:21.

MOTHER called us children from our play one July evening to eat a ripe, cold watermelon. Everyone was delighted at the invitation except Johnny and me.

"Johnny shouldn't have any watermelon," I pouted. "He doesn't play fair."

"I do too!" countered Johnny. "You're the one who cheated."

Mother interrupted, "Children, children! That isn't a kind way to talk."

"But Johnny doesn't play fair," I repeated.

Mother ignored my charge. Pointing to the watermelon on the table, she asked me, "What color is this watermelon?"

"Anyone can see that it's green," I answered.

Mother then took a knife and cut the watermelon in two and held one half so that we could see the ripe, red center. "What color is the melon, Johnny?" she asked.

"It's red," said Johnny.

"One said the melon was green. The other said it was red. You disagree, yet both of you are correct. Always remember that the other fellow can be right even though he doesn't agree with you."

Most disagreements arise because we do not think of the other fellow. Are you willing to consider your friend's feelings when you disagree with him? Would you like to ask God to help you keep from quarreling with your friends when things go wrong?

FAMILY PRAYER: *Dear God, help us to work and play in peace, and to be tolerant of those who disagree with us. Amen.*

TWENTIETH DAY OF THE MONTH

We Pray For
RESPONSIBILITY

He shall reward every man according to his works.
—MATTHEW 16:27.

ONCE when Father found a runt among the newborn pigs in the barn-yard, he appointed us children its keeper and charged us to feed it regularly. A runt was a baby pig, so small and weak that it could not care for itself.

What fun we had sitting on the cob pile, feeding the little pig warm milk from a spoon! The little pig soon learned that we were his friends, and he followed us wherever we went, grunting for food.

Having a pet wasn't all play, however. Feeding the little fellow five times a day and providing him a clean, comfortable home often proved to be work.

When at last the little pig had grown big and strong, Father turned him back into the barnyard. "My children, you have done your work well," he said. "When I sell this pig at market, I will give the money to you."

God expects us to do our part that we may deserve some of the joys He has planned for us. If we want beautiful flowers in our yard, we must plant and cultivate them. If we want pets, we must accept the responsibility of feeding and caring for them. If we cross a street or highway, we must accept our responsibility and obey the traffic laws. What are some of your responsibilities at home, at school and at church? Would you like to ask God to help you work without grumbling?

FAMILY PRAYER: *We love, dear God, to work with You. Help us to do our share to make this world a happy place. Amen.*

TWENTY-FIRST DAY OF THE MONTH

We Pray For
RESPECT

Do unto others as you would have them do unto you.
—MATTHEW 7:12.

FROM the time that we were old enough to understand, Mother instructed us to respect each other's property. It was a family law that we must ask permission before using anything that belonged to another.

I remember that some children who came to visit us pulled our playthings from the shelves and handled them so roughly that we were almost in tears. Mother came to our rescue by taking us out to the barn to see some little kittens. Then she returned to the house to lay our toys carefully away.

That night Mother called a family conference. "It is not right for others to mistreat the toys that you value, children. But we must also be kind to our guests. What shall be done about it?"

After much discussion, Father suggested this plan: "Each of you select one toy that Mother can keep in a box in the kitchen. Whenever your friends come, they may play with the things you have provided; but you do not have to share your most valued toys unless you wish."

Father's plan worked perfectly. Thereafter, those children who respected property were invited to share our treasured things. The others were invited to play only with the toys in the kitchen.

Do you respect the property of others at home, at school, at the homes of your playmates? Would you like to ask God to help you be as careful with your friends' toys as you are with your own?

FAMILY PRAYER: *Dear God, Your wisdom and love in our heart help us to know what is good and fair that we may do unto others as we would have them do unto us. Amen.*

TWENTY-SECOND DAY OF THE MONTH

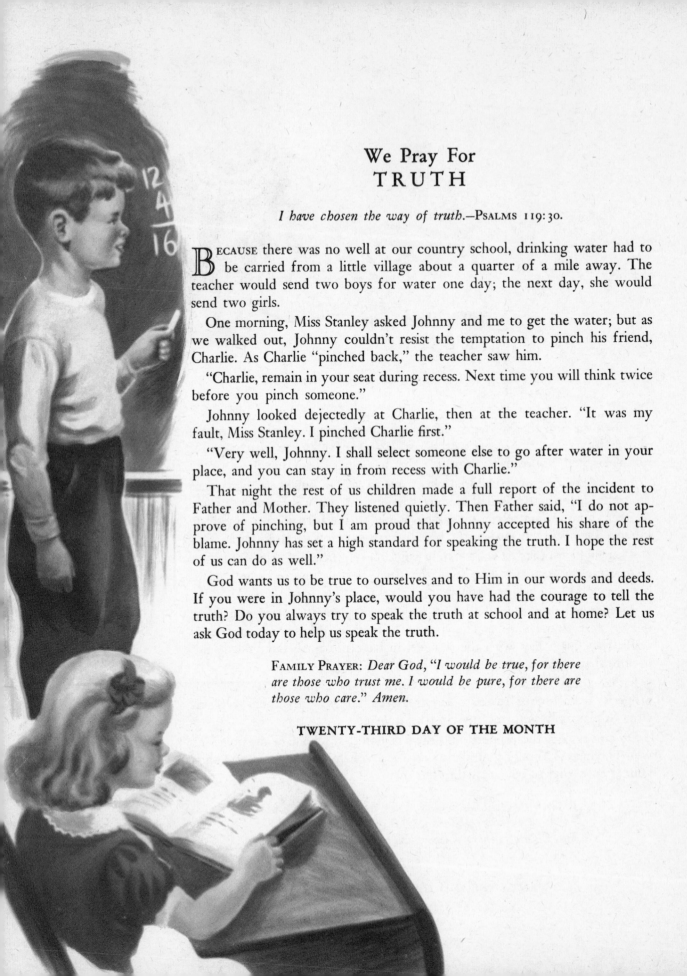

We Pray For
TRUTH

I have chosen the way of truth.—PSALMS 119:30.

BECAUSE there was no well at our country school, drinking water had to be carried from a little village about a quarter of a mile away. The teacher would send two boys for water one day; the next day, she would send two girls.

One morning, Miss Stanley asked Johnny and me to get the water; but as we walked out, Johnny couldn't resist the temptation to pinch his friend, Charlie. As Charlie "pinched back," the teacher saw him.

"Charlie, remain in your seat during recess. Next time you will think twice before you pinch someone."

Johnny looked dejectedly at Charlie, then at the teacher. "It was my fault, Miss Stanley. I pinched Charlie first."

"Very well, Johnny. I shall select someone else to go after water in your place, and you can stay in from recess with Charlie."

That night the rest of us children made a full report of the incident to Father and Mother. They listened quietly. Then Father said, "I do not approve of pinching, but I am proud that Johnny accepted his share of the blame. Johnny has set a high standard for speaking the truth. I hope the rest of us can do as well."

God wants us to be true to ourselves and to Him in our words and deeds. If you were in Johnny's place, would you have had the courage to tell the truth? Do you always try to speak the truth at school and at home? Let us ask God today to help us speak the truth.

FAMILY PRAYER: *Dear God, "I would be true, for there are those who trust me. I would be pure, for there are those who care." Amen.*

TWENTY-THIRD DAY OF THE MONTH

We Pray For
WISDOM

Give me understanding that I may learn Thy commandments.—PSALMS 119:73.

ONE of our favorite Bible stories was about the wisest man who ever lived. Almost every week, one of us children would ask Mother to tell us the story of the wise man, Solomon. Then Mother would begin:

"Once there was a man named Solomon, who had just been made king of his people. And Solomon prayed to God: 'I am only a child, O Lord. I know not how to rule this great people. Give me wisdom and knowledge, O Lord, that I may judge for my people and may know how to rule them rightly.'

"It pleased the Lord that Solomon had asked this thing. And the Lord told Solomon, 'Since you have not asked for a long life, nor great riches for yourself, nor victory over your enemies, nor great power, but have asked for wisdom and knowledge to judge your people, I shall give you wisdom greater than that of any king before you and greater than that of any king that shall come after you. Also, I shall give you that for which you did not ask, riches and honor. And if you will obey my words as David, your father did, you shall have a long life and shall rule for many years.'

"And Solomon kept God's commandments and he was known as the wisest man who ever lived." (*II Chronicles* 1:7-13.)

We learn to speak by listening to others. We learn to sing by listening to others. How much more important it is that we learn of God's wisdom by listening to God. If we listen when we pray, God will help us think of new ways to love and serve and understand others. Would you like to pray today, asking God to help you recognize the difference between right and wrong?

FAMILY PRAYER: *Open our hearts and minds, O God.*
Fill us with understanding that we may know Thy
work to be done. Amen.

TWENTY-FOURTH DAY OF THE MONTH

We Pray For
CLEANLINESS

Create in me a clean heart, O God; and renew a right
spirit within me.—PSALMS 51:10.

MOTHER believed that "cleanliness is next to godliness," so we took baths on Saturday night to be ready for church on Sunday. When we were young, we couldn't take a bath every day as you do.

First, we didn't have hot and cold running water, and it took a great deal of "fixin'" to heat the bath water on the cookstove. Secondly, we didn't have bathrooms in our homes, so we had to bathe in a big, round wooden washtub that we set in the kitchen.

On Saturday nights, after supper dishes had been cleared away, Father built an extra hot fire in the cookstove to warm the room and to heat the kettles of water that had been carried from the well. Then, with the window shades tightly drawn, we children were ushered into the kitchen, one by one, to take our turns in the tub. There was much "ohing" and "ahing" because the water was either too hot or too cold; but despite our protests, Mother saw that we were well scrubbed. Wise as she was, she made us understand that clean bodies help us to have clean thoughts.

We keep our bodies clean with soap and water. We keep our thoughts and words clean by thinking true, kind, and loving thoughts. Would you like to ask God to help you have clean thoughts all day long?

FAMILY PRAYER: *O God, we come to You to learn right*
from wrong in all that we do and say. Amen.

TWENTY-FIFTH DAY OF THE MONTH

We Pray For
SELF CONTROL

Let every man be quick to hear, slow to speak, slow to anger.—JAMES 1:19.

THERE is a time to speak and a time to keep silence, but we children had a difficult time learning the difference. Often we caused Mother and Father and ourselves considerable embarrassment because we were quick to express our opinions about things and people. I remember hearing Mother and Father tell us, "If you can't say anything good about a person, you shouldn't say anything at all."

On the first page of an autograph album I received for Christmas one year, Mother had written: "If wisdom's ways you wisely seek, five things observe with care: To whom you speak, of whom you speak, and how and when and where."

On the second page was this terse advice from Father: "Think twice, and then keep it to yourself."

Because God gave us the ability to speak, we are apt to think that we must talk constantly. Often we can say most by saying nothing—particularly if we are angry. People are often sorry for the things they said when they were angry. Would you like to ask God to help you keep silent whenever you are tempted to speak unkindly?

FAMILY PRAYER: *May all we think or do or say please You, dear God, in every way. Amen.*

TWENTY-SIXTH DAY OF THE MONTH

We Pray For
LOYALTY

Lo, I am with you always, even unto the end of the world.—MATTHEW 28:30.

ONE of Father's favorite stories concerned a wild duck that fell near a farmer's barnyard, because of a broken wing. The farmer was filled with pity for he knew that the mother duck would never fly again. He mended the bird's wing and gave her food and shelter in his barnyard.

All through the winter the mother duck was lonely. She called to each flock of wild ducks that passed over, but she received no answer to her call.

One spring morning a single duck appeared in the sky. The mother duck called, just as she had done a hundred times before; but on this occasion, an answering call came back. Her mate, a beautiful mallard with purple and green markings, had found her at last.

How happy and excited was the mother duck as she squeezed through the fence and hurried toward the pond in the pasture to meet her mate! There they lived happily all summer, growing fat on succulent reeds and insects, and rearing a family of noisy ducklings.

When the weather turned cold in the fall, the mallard bade his mate farewell, and with the young birds, he flew back to the southland for the winter. The mother duck then returned to the farmer's barnyard, but no longer was she sad. She knew that her mate would return the next spring and every spring thereafter.

All birds and animals are loyal to those whom they love. A puppy loves you even though you hurt him. He forgives you even though you forget to feed him. He stays with you even though others leave you. How can we be loyal to our friends, our home, and God? Would you like to ask God to help you remain loyal to your friends even though they forget you?

FAMILY PRAYER: *O God, bless us with loyal hearts, and keep us loving and kind to one another. Amen.*

TWENTY-SEVENTH DAY OF THE MONTH

We Pray For
PROTECTION

He commands even wind and water, and they obey Him.—LUKE 8:25.

AFTER we children had taken our baths and were in bed one Saturday night, a great storm blew out of the southwest with heavy rain and roar of thunder. In a short time the strong winds grew into a dangerous, twisting tornado, uprooting trees and buildings in its path.

Mother and Father saw the storm coming, and, as they prayed, they acted quickly. Arousing us children, they led us to the storm cellar in the back yard where we would be safe. But just as the storm rushed over the hills toward our home, a strange thing happened. The tornado suddenly swept up into the air and passed over our farm without disturbing even one twig on a tree. And there in the storm cellar Father led us in prayer, giving thanks to God for His protection.

Our help comes from God, who made heaven and earth. When we are afraid, we will trust in Him, who neither slumbers nor sleeps, for He is our keeper. He watches over us forever. Can you think of a prayer to thank God for protecting us from dangers?

FAMILY PRAYER: *We thank You, Father, for keeping us safe in your protecting love. Amen.*

TWENTY-EIGHTH DAY OF THE MONTH

We Pray For
COOPERATION

The Lord is my helper.—HEBREWS 13:6.

WHEN Father bought us children a pony, we took excellent care of her and provided her with all the luxuries a pony could want. We were Daisy's friend, certainly, but there was some doubt whether Daisy was our friend. She appeared restless and shy whenever we came near.

That night as we prepared for bed, we said our prayers, ending with a plea, "Dear God, please don't let Daisy run away."

That was too much for Father! He asked us to dress and follow him to the barn. There in the stable as he held the lantern high, Father explained, "Children, it is not God's responsibility to keep Daisy from running away. It's yours. See that the barn door is closed so that your pony can't get out. God can't do your work for you."

When we returned to the house, Father asked us to pray again. This time, at his suggestion, we said, "Thank you, God, for our pony. Help us remember to keep the barn door shut so Daisy won't run away."

Is it God's responsibility or yours to keep your puppy out of the street, to keep your money safe in your pocket, to keep your bicycle out of the rain? Would you like to ask God to help you remember to obey the traffic lights when you cross the streets?

FAMILY PRAYER: *Dear God, help us to do our share in making possible many of the joys and protections that You have planned for us. Amen.*

TWENTY-NINTH DAY OF THE MONTH

We Pray For
FAITH

And God said, Let the earth bring forth grass . . .
*and it was so.—*GENESIS 1:11.

BURNING off the pasture land was a thrilling experience of our childhood on the farm. On a spring day when there was no wind to fan the fire, Father invited the neighbors to come for an early supper that Mother had prepared; then all of us went to the pasture to burn away the old grass.

Mounted on a horse, Father rode across one end of the field, dragging behind him a firebrand to ignite the dead weeds. Men followed with rakes and shovels to tend the flames that ate their way across the pasture. Nearby were buckets and tubs of water that had been hauled from the well just in the event that the fire should suddenly get out of control.

The crackle of the burning weeds and the smell of the smoke delighted us children. But when the work was finished and we beheld the entire pasture burned black and crisp, we doubted the grass would ever grow there again.

Our fears were ill-founded, however. Within a week or two, green grass and spring flowers spread over the meadow like a beautiful carpet. The fire had cleared away the rubbish so that new grass could grow.

God asks us to have faith and to believe that in Him all things are possible. When we call our friends on the telephone, we have faith that they will answer. When we turn on an electric light, we have faith that it will burn. When we turn on the radio, we have faith that it will broadcast. By faith, we know that the world was created by God, and we do not doubt that He will always love and care for us. By faith, we know that we will be united with Him in heaven. Let us ask God to help us have faith in the things that we do not understand and cannot see.

> FAMILY PRAYER: *Give us eyes to see the glory of Your creation, O God. Give us faith to understand that all things are possible with You. Amen.*

THIRTIETH DAY OF THE MONTH